I0060729

How To Irritate A Telemarketer

SIDNEY S. PRASAD

Copyright © 2014 Sidney S. Prasad

All rights reserved.

ISBN: 1927676347
ISBN-13:978-1-927676-34-9

DEDICATION

This book is dedicated to my great friend Tina Patel.

CONTENTS

ACKNOWLEDGMENTS

When was the last time you irritated a telemarketer?

1 REVENGE

Inform the telemarketer that you are a private investigator and they just called a murder scene.

Tell the telemarketer that you don't do business on the telephone. Then excuse yourself and say you have to call Pizza Hut and order dinner.

Respond by saying, "your mama" after every question.

Ask the telemarketer to send you some information in the mail. In the event they give you a follow up call, tell them that you are illiterate.

Tap your car and make the alarm go off, then stick your phone on the hood.

Ask the telemarketer to Google the Do Not Call Registry and get you their phone number. Then ask for a callback in 10 minutes and tell them to enjoy the fine.

As soon as the telemarketer identifies themselves say, "Shhhh." Keeping shushing them until they hang up.

Listen to the telemarketer's entire pitch and say, "bullshit!"

Pretend to have Tourette syndrome by alternating normal speech to swearing obnoxiously.

Ask the telemarketer what they want to do when they grow up.

2 NOW WE'RE EVEN

Continuously ask the telemarketer to repeat themselves.

Lift a second phone receiver and record the telemarketer live as they are pitching you. Then freak them out by playing their voice back.

If the representative is attempting to conduct a telephone survey, ask them the following; "I have a survey question for you, how many times has someone told you to fuck off today?"

Tell the telemarketer that you are just browsing and hang-up.

If the telemarketer is a female keep saying, "yes Sir" and if it's a male keep saying, "yes Ma'am."

Whisper back all of your responses and refuse to talk in a normal monotone.

Kindly explain to the telemarketer that you will indeed subscribe to their service provided that they send 1000 satisfied client testimonials within the next 5 minutes.

Be a bullshit artist and claim that their competitors just offered you the exact same package 50% off their price.

Stick your telephone in the microwave, closed the door and don't turn it on. Let the telemarketer listen to the echoes of how silly they sound.

Give the telemarketer crap and accuse them off just calling 5 minutes ago.

Pretend to be an answering machine.

Each time the telemarketer asks you a question respond in a sexual moaning tone.

Tell the telemarketer that you are unemployed and ask them if their company is hiring.

Remain silent and don't say a word until the telemarketer hangs up.

Contentiously interrupt the telemarketer and claim that you don't understand them because they are talking too fast.

Respond to each of the telemarketer's questions by saying, "I can't tell you but I can tell you my pin number."

Request for a callback at midnight as most state regulations prohibit telemarketing calls after 9:00 PM.

Tell the telemarketer that you're in the middle of a robbery and decided to pick up the phone.

4 WHAT'S YOUR NUMBER?

Stick your phone next to the toilet and flush it a couple of times.

Mimic everything the telemarketer says verbatim.

Tell the telemarketer that you're a squatter and have no decision making authority.

Ask the telemarketer what color their underwear is. Then ask them for some proof.

Request a quote minus the telemarketer's hourly wage or commission.

Request to be transferred to the telemarketer's supervisor. Then ask to be transferred to the supervisor's supervisor. Once you get to the top of the totem pole request to be transferred to the initial telemarketer.

Ask the telemarketer if it's their first day because they sound really shitty.

Interrupt the telemarketer by dialing your home phone number from your cell phone.

Ask the telemarketer to give you random fast food restaurant phone numbers until they give up on you.

Tell the telemarketer that you need a loan and if it's ok that you don't pay them back.

Give the telemarketer a complex by continuously asking for their name. Laugh like a school girl each time they say their name.

Ask the telemarketer if they're interested in engaging into some friendly phone sex with you.

In the event the telemarketer is promoting long distance plans, ask them the rates for several different countries.

Respond to all the telemarketer's questions in a foreign language.

Put a porn movie on and stick the phone next to the speakers.

Ask the telemarketer if they want to hear a really cool sound and then hang up on them.

Be a chunky butt and eat an entire meal as the telemarketer delivers their pitch.

Crumple a piece of paper into the telephone receiver and yell, "sorry bad connection."

Pretend to be a dumb redneck and answer back using the following phrases:

Huh?

Say what now?

Come again?

Request to be removed off the telemarketer's calling and mailing list but not to remove you from Santa's list.

Listen to the telemarketer's entire sales pitch then identify yourself as a telephone auditor hired by their firm. Ask the telemarketer to speak a little slower on their next couple of calls and maybe stand up when they pitch to get better vocal projections.

Say, "blah, blah, blah" each time the telemarketer says something.

Put a screaming baby on the phone for the telemarketer to listen to.

Work out a routine with your roommate and get them to pick up the phone every 20 seconds and say, "are you done yet man?" Each time the telemarketer questions you if it's a bad time say you have some time to kill and it's convenient right now.

Listen to the telemarketer's pitch and say, "thank you," then hang up.

Ask the telemarketer what gender they are.

Give the telemarketer shit for interrupting your internet porn night.

Turn into a Negative Nelly and pour your heart out to the telemarketer for an hour.

Ask the telemarketer if they enjoy bugging the shit out of people for a living.

Ask the telemarketer if you can call them at home from your work tomorrow.

Inquire about the most expensive product or service that the telemarketer is promoting. Then get them to hold on while you count your pennies one-by-one.

Repeatedly say, "I forgive you" each time the telemarketer makes a statement.

Kindly inform the telemarketer that you are 98 years old and anxiously waiting for the Grim Reaper.

Request for a callback the following day when you will have your TeleZapper installed.

If you recognize the telemarketer's phone number, then answer the phone like this: "Good Evening Sleazy Susan's Sex Line all calls $2.95 per minute."

Ask the telemarketer to spell each item that they're pitching you on.

Crank the volume on your television set and filter out the telemarketer's voice.

Keep referring to the telemarketer as a "telephone hooker."

Place the telemarketer on hold for 2 hours.

Give the telemarketer the name and phone number of your pesky neighbor and say they're your landlord who makes the major decisions.

Regardless of how old you are, tell the telemarketer that you are a minor and disqualified from making major decisions.

Blatantly lie and tell the telemarketer that you don't own a phone.

If the telemarketer sounds like they're out of breath, then ask them if they just finished playing with themselves.

Tell the telemarketer that you work in the exact same company as them and it's against the company rules for them to solicit you.

Push all the buttons on your telephone pad simultaneously until the telemarketer hangs up.

Ask the telemarketer for their call center address and then question every possible landmark description in their vicinity.

9 WHY ME?

Like a broken record keep saying, "no" until the telemarketer discontinues the call.

Pretend that you are hard of hearing and ask the telemarketer to raise their voice a couple of times. Then request to be transferred to their supervisor and complain that their representative was screaming at you.

Ask a bunch of personal questions with no limitations of the content.

Pretend that you have a bunch of hostages captive and you thought the telemarketer was the negotiator.

Listen to the telemarketer's sales pitch and ask them to quote their rate in a dozen different foreign currencies.

Listen to the telemarketer's pitch and say, "me no English."

Request for a callback in a decade because you just got sentenced today for a 10 year jail term for mismanaging a daycare.

Ask the telemarketer their name, their mother's name, and go up their entire family tree until they hang up.

Each time the telemarketer makes a statement, respond by saying, "that's not true."

10 BONUS CHAPTER PREVIEW: HOW TO PISS OFF A SALESMAN

Open the door and boldly ask the salesman if this is his sick idea of a knock knock joke. Then slam the door before he can answer you.

Don't answer the door, but violently start knocking on the other side of the door.

Take your clothes off and
answer the door nude.

Answer the door with a couple of boxes in your hand. Then ask the salesman if he will help you move.

Listen to the sales presentation while passionately scratching your crotch area.

Interrupt the sales presentation and repeatedly ask questions about the return policy.

Stick a lighter by your smoke detector and make your fire alarm go off prior to answering the door. Then run outside, waving your arms and yell, "fire."

Open the door and scream, "pervert, rape, sicko," at the top of your lungs.

Answer the door and ask the salesman if they came for the strip poker game.

CONCLUSION

There are a million different things we can do to irritate telemarketers ranging from giving our telephones a swirly or reaching for the closest musical instrument. I'm not suggesting to imitate any of the scenarios mentioned in this book, as telemarketers are human, or somewhat human in their own way. I wrote this book as pure entertainment for my readers and don't want to get anyone in trouble. Just to be safe maybe let your answering machine pick any unidentified callers for the next little while.

ABOUT THE AUTHOR

Sidney S. Prasad is an author on a quest to make the world laugh. His work is focused on entertaining people with his dry-humored novels. Sidney S. Prasad personally believes laughter is the best cure for all of life's ups and downs.

Some other humorous books written by Sidney S. Prasad include:

How To Piss Off A Telemarketer,
How To Piss Off A Salesman
My Bipolar Manager,
Don't Ask Dumb Questions!,
Corny Names & Stupid Places,
Misfortune Cookies,
My Stupid CEO,
Plenty Of Freaks: Are You Sold On Online Dating?
Plenty Of Freaks: Worst Online Dating Mistakes
Plenty Of Freaks: Is Dating Legalized Prostitution?
and
Telemarketer's Revenge: The Customer Is Always Wrong, Bitch!

www.ingramcontent.com/pod-product-compliance
Lightning Source LLC
Chambersburg PA
CBHW060629210326
41520CB00010B/1532